Agile Project Management

The Step by Step Guide that You Must Have to Learn Project Management Correctly from the Beginning to the End

Eric Thompson

Disclaimer Notice:

Please note the information contained within this document is for educational and entertainment purposes only. All effort has been executed to present accurate, up to date, and reliable, complete information. No warranties of any kind are declared or implied. Readers acknowledge that the author is not engaging in the rendering of legal, financial, medical or professional advice. The content within this book has been derived from various sources. Please consult a licensed professional before attempting any techniques outlined in this book.

By reading this document, the reader agrees that under no circumstances is the author responsible for any losses, direct or indirect, which are incurred as a result of the use of information contained within this document, including, but not limited to, — errors, omissions, or inaccuracies.

Table of Contents

Chapter 1: Introduction to Agile Project Management Method

In the management field, everyone manages projects. Whether one is a certified manager or not, at one point, they had to manage their projects to ensure that the end product delivered meets the customer requirements. Unfortunately, most managers manage their projects by "winging it." Often, this results in struggles to effectively manage multiple projects at once or to beat deadlines and also to adapt to the ever-changing project requirements. In a bid to solve the project management challenges faced by most people, companies utilize varying standard project management methodologies.

With regards to the above, the best way of mitigating challenges associated with project management is to adopt a project management technique that works. However, with the numerous methods out there, it becomes a daunting task to choose one. Most individuals would have a difficult time determining the best method that works for them. Fortunately, this book will guide you through agile project management methodology as one of the best strategies you can use to manage your projects.

So, what is agile? Agile refers to project management techniques which use short development cycles referred to as "sprints" to put a major focus on continuous enhancement during the development of a product or service. Essentially, agile is a method used to manage projects. This method of project management can be utilized for any project management process. However, it was basically founded to help in software development.

Back in the day, industries used conventional approaches to manage their projects. During this period, companies used methods such as the earned value management or the PERT method to coordinate project tasks. As global economies changed, there was a shift in the focus of what should be delivered to the end customer. Earlier on, the importance of quality and doing it right was a major emphasis. With the changing times, new management techniques evolved. Doing things right was no longer good enough. Companies must now learn to get things done on time.

Without a doubt, the customers' desire to get their products or services on time has changed the way companies do business. Unfortunately, if one company fails to meet the timely demands of their customers, then their rivals in the market will meet the need. Having mentioned this, project managers in companies need to wake up and appreciate the changes going on around them. In other words, they need to be more agile.

The advent of the internet also came with changes, more so in the way in which businesses handle project management activities. Today, companies need to embrace the importance of using project management methods such as agile. The term "agile" is defined as "able to move quickly and easily." From this definition, project managers are expected to adjust quickly to their changing environments. In this case, they should rapidly adjust to the changing needs of customers.

The introduction of the internet has led to numerous uncertainties when dealing with projects. Most project managers will attest that it is nearly impossible to keep up with all the changes in any project management process. It is after a project starts that a customer realizes that they did not want exactly what they had initially requested. Unfortunately, the costs to any business for such rapid changes are immense. This mostly applies when projects are not completed in time or rather when the end product or service does not meet the requirements of consumers. An approach that strives to deal with such unpredictabilities while acknowledging the importance of learning in the project life cycle should, therefore, be utilized in any organization. This approach is what is termed "agile project management."

History of Agile

As mentioned earlier, agile project management was initially developed as a way of helping in software development. During the early 1990s, when PC computing began to take shape in most industries, software development went through a major crisis. During this period, the crisis was referred to as "application delivery lag." Just as the name suggests, the industry faced a huge problem of delivering software within a short time-frame. The time that it took for any business to get their actual application to be produced was about three years.

The issue was that businesses moved faster than application development. Therefore, this led to a scenario where projects could end up being canceled, as they were no longer needed, considering the time lag. As a result of the failures, people grew frustrated with the process. An aerospace engineer in the 90s, Jon Kern was one who was greatly disappointed in the process. With time, Kern and other software thought leaders pushed for the adoption of better software development processes.

Following their propositions, there were major changes. For instance, earlier on, the automotive industry took about six years to design a new car. During the 90s, this time was reduced by almost half of the time it initially took. With the frustrations that surrounded the unproductive software development activities, this led to the notable Snowbird meeting held in Utah in 2001. This was the second time this group met after their initial meeting in 2000. During their conference, agile was not their primary goal. In fact, at the time, other terms were being used to refer to the practice, including "lightweight" and "light."

In particular, the software thought leaders had an aim of quickly developing software and getting it into the hands of consumers. There were numerous benefits associated with such fast software delivery. Users could enjoy the benefits of the software much faster. Also, the software development team benefited as they gained rapid feedback on the software's functionality.

It is through the benefits such as the rapid feedback and the overall willingness to change that formed the key aspects of the agile movement.

Advantages of Agile Project Management

With regards to project management, there are several advantages that project teams, project leaders, sponsors, and customers gain through the use of agile. To clearly understand how agile is beneficial to project management, it is vital to comprehend what is meant by the term "project management."

The process of managing any project is a challenging task when a company fails to know all the areas where they need to work. For a project to succeed, it depends on individual sections being put together to function optimally. One of the main reasons why projects fail is because of the misalignment existing between the business strategy and the project goals. A project could also fail because of the absence of executive support or sponsorship. Equally, it could flounder because of existing vague business goals and requirements. These are just a few of the reasons why most projects fail.

To ensure that a project thrives, identify the people, processes, techniques, and vital technologies that are required for success. Bearing this in mind, project management is defined as the bringing together of processes, skills, knowledge, techniques, and input and output utilized by project managers to complete a project.

Some of the basic project management goals that any strategic body should push to achieve:

- Creating a framework which shows that the PMO and EPMO align to enterprise objectives.

- Providing senior managers with valuable information.

- Getting the right personnel, knowledge, and skills.

- Reporting on important areas the business cares about.

- Identifying PMO and EPMO achievements.

Successful project management requires more than just the technical know-how of an individual. There are other non-technical skills that good managers ought to portray, as well. An ideal project manager should have soft skills such as leadership, communication, prioritization, organization, problem-solving, adaptability, and motivation.

It is also worth noting that the project management process is divided into five different phases, including:

- Initiation

- Planning

- Executing

- Monitoring and controlling

- Closing

Now, applying the agile project management method to any project management activity has many advantages. Some of them are discussed below.

Enhanced Product Quality

Using agile project management ensures that the end quality of any product or service is improved. It is worth noting that agile advocates for the idea of testing a product at every stage of its lifecycle. This implies that the regular checkups are there to make sure that the product is functional even during developmental stages. In line with this, the product owner can easily make the necessary changes to the product. The result is a product that meets the customer demands in every angle.

Agile methods bring ideal safeguards against product problems. For instance, the agile method fosters a proactive approach aimed at preventing complications related to the product. Equally, agile embraces technological excellence and sustainable development as part of producing a quality product to meet clients' demands. The agile method helps the management team define and elaborate on requirements quickly enough to guarantee that the product features are relevant to customers' expectations.

During the development process, a product also goes through daily testing and continuous integration. As a result, the development team is in a better position to address product issues while they are still fresh. This helps a lot as there are minimal to no delays if there are any changes or issues that need addressing.

Higher Customer Satisfaction

Using the agile method also leads to higher customer satisfaction. This is easily gained since the product owner is fully involved during the product development process. The product owner knows more about product requirements and customer expectations. Consequently, keeping them involved guarantees that the final product meets customer demands. Ultimately, consumers are more likely to be pleased with the product delivered to them.

Besides involving the product owner, the agile method also engages the customer throughout the project. This means that there is a high probability that the product will feature what the customer wants. Higher customer satisfaction is also achieved by ensuring that the product backlog is constantly prioritized and updated to help product developers in responding quickly to change.

Customers are also frequently updated on the product's functionality during every step of the development process. Certainly, this also aids in minimizing last-minute changes, which often affects the delivery of the final product. Ultimately, the agile method aids in delivering a product fast enough to capitalize on the existing market demand. With these changes as a result of using the agile method, customers are pleased not only with the fast delivery of products but also for the quality of products that they get in the market.

Higher Team Morale

The idea of working with a self-managing team creates a working environment where people are innovative and creative. The best part is that individuals are also credited for their expertise. Concerning this benefit, a project manager is there to remove existing impediments in the development team. As such, there would be no external interference. Bearing in mind that there are different functional areas all with a similar purpose, these people will learn new skills. With time, they get to enhance their skills by learning from other people on the team.

Increased Collaboration

The cross-functional team using the agile method regularly works closely together. Scrum meetings held daily allow the development team to organize work effectively by planning future assignments, while at the same time dealing with development roadblocks. The scrum master, the product owner, and the development team also communicate frequently with the stakeholders during sprint reviews. This fosters increased collaboration among all parties linked to the product being developed.

More Relevant Metrics

Comparing the metrics used by agile project teams to those which were conventionally used, the metrics utilized by the agile project teams are more accurate and relevant. In most cases, these metrics aid inaccurate estimation of the time the project will take to complete, the cost of the project, and its overall performance. Accordingly, this leads to better decisions.

Enhanced Performance Visibility

The best thing about agile projects is that team

members have the opportunity to understand how the project is coming along at every stage. This is possible through the daily sprint reviews and daily scrum meetings. Visible charts are also offered as a concrete way of seeing the project's progress. Therefore, there is improved performance visibility. No one is left in the dark during the product's development process.

Increased Project Control

Using agile project management creates numerous opportunities for the team to constantly inspect the project. This means that team members have a better way of exercising control of the project, in addition to regular sprint meetings. The fact that every team player is aware of the project's progress implies that there is transparency on how things are done.

Improved Project Predictability

While having better-increased project control, there is also improved project predictability through the many tools and practices utilized by the project's team. For instance, it is possible to predict how much the project will cost and the length of time it takes to complete it. The information gained from daily scrum meetings helps the team to easily predict the likely performance of the product in the market.

Reduced Risk

Using agile methodologies ensure that the risks of absolute project failure are eliminated. The idea is to have a working product right from the first sprint. Developing a product in sprints guarantees that the entire project never completely fails. If there is anything that should be changed, then this can easily be done by sorting a particular sprint and not abandoning the entire project.

Also, at every stage of the development, the project is tailored to meet the requirements of the customer. This implies that usable features are incorporated as a way of making sure that the product being developed is relevant. As such, this minimizes the likelihood of project failure.

Besides, there are also self-funding projects utilized to generate revenue early. Therefore, organizations get to fund a project with little up-front expense. The notion of a project failing for lack of funds is eliminated.

Faster ROI

The advantages of a product being developed can be experienced even during the development stages. This implies that the organization can easily witness quick returns on investment (ROI). Agile means that a product is delivered to the market quickly. As a result, if there are any changes required by customers, this can be done promptly. The advantage is that an organization using agile gains a competitive advantage over other companies fighting for the same market.

There is a good reason why organizations should utilize this method to manage their projects. The fact that a product is delivered faster to the market implies that the time to market is also quick and efficient. The agile project team is productive. The organization, therefore, stands a chance to gain a competitive edge over rivals in the market. Agile project management leads to enhanced product quality delivered to the market.

The Main Principles of Agile Project Management

A deeper look into agile management reveals the fact that there are principles which govern how to run a project. In other words, it tells a lot about how an agile project should be handled. There are 12 principles of agile project management.

1. The highest priority is to meet customer requirements through rapid and

continuous delivery.

2. Changes are acknowledged at any stage of product development.

3. A higher frequency of delivery of product or service is embraced.

4. Stakeholders and developers work together closely during the development of the product or service.

5. The project is built around a group of motivated people.

6. Face-to-face interactions are regarded as the most effective form of communication.

7. A working product is the primary measure of success.

8. Agile processes advocate for sustainable development.

9. Agility is enhanced through ongoing

attention to detail, good design, and excellence.

10. Simplicity is a vital element.

11. The use of self-organizing teams leads to the development of ideal architectures and designs which aid in meeting requirements.

12. Regular intervals are utilized to inspect and adapt to guarantee effectiveness.

A look into these principles reveals that the principles act as guidance on how different people can collaborate and work toward a common goal. There are many topics that these principles touch on, including people interactions, management behavior, team behavior, continuous improvement, and measuring progress. More about the principles of agile project management is discussed in the next chapter.

Chapter 2: Understand the Principles of Agile Project Management

Generally, the best way to understand what agile is is that it is a way of managing projects. Well, the method was first introduced to help in software development. And agile can be used in any organization. Companies often have to handle projects that deliver products and services to their customers. To guarantee that these projects run smoothly, people need to interact with each other in the best way possible. The team working on the project should also collaborate effectively. More importantly, the project's progress should be monitored constantly for the best performance. The agile method helps to achieve all these. This method governs how a project is handled. The 12 agile project management principles will be discussed in detail here.

Customer Satisfaction

The first principle of the agile method is customer satisfaction. The aim of a project manager should be to deliver a product or service which solves problems. Customer satisfaction is not only met through delivering quality products but also delivering the product on time and ensuring that continuous delivery of the product is maintained. This, therefore, calls for minimizing the time taken in each step of product development. The project manager should work to make the development process more efficient. Implementing the agile method makes sure that unnecessary activities are cut down to meet the customer's requirements.

Making and Managing Changes

One of the biggest benefits gained by using the agile project management method is that it gives the project manager the flexibility they need with regards to change. In comparison to other project management methods, it might be difficult to make changes depending on the project development phase. For instance, it would be hard to make necessary changes at the late development stages. However, the agile project management method makes this possible.

How can agile method help in making changes even in the late stages of the project development cycle? Well, customers are always changing their minds. New technology could be introduced in the market, and customers expect this technology to be incorporated into the product. Consequently, you need to adjust accordingly. This is what agile is all about. If you chose to release a product in the market and ignored the customer demands, this could be a waste of money. In the end, you would release an obsolete technology. With the help of the agile project management method, you can effectively make changes which will guarantee that the product being released is what the customers want. There are several ways in which agile can help manage changes throughout the product development process.

Continuous Customer Input

A major benefit of the agile method is that it allows customer input at every stage of product development. Therefore, the development team can use customer feedback sooner rather than later. If the customer wants new features, these are considered and changes made immediately.

Priorities Set through Product Backlog

The agile method fosters a collaborative environment where the customers and the whole project development team can bring input toward what should be prioritized. Since all members can add anything to the product's backlog, this means that changes can be made and priorities attended to in an ideal manner.

Effective Communication through Daily Meetings

Ideally, the best way to handle frequent changes throughout the product development process is through daily meetings at about the same time. The significance of these meetings is that members have an opportunity to discuss tasks related to the project. This means that they can also talk about existing obstacles and ways to mitigate them.

These meetings can help a lot in discussing the product's requirements. Regular discussions can help in dealing with changes within the shortest time possible.

Task Handling through Task Boards

Traditionally, the project's team would know about the product requirements by reading requirements documents. Often these papers are overlooked as they are simply read once and left in the mailbox. With agile, tasks are divided using a task board. This board divides assignments into different columns, and they are visible 24/7. The visibility gained through the use of the task board makes it easy to change requirements.

Making and managing changes is part of any project demands. A development team must have a plan to handle how these changes will be solved. The agile method gives the project development team an ideal platform for dealing with these changes. Ultimately, it is by making changes effectively that a product meets clients' demands is delivered to the market.

Shorter Timescale

The third agile project management principle relates to the idea of delivering a product within a shorter timescale. Earlier, the process of developing a product was mostly consumed with documentation. For instance, in software development, major emphasis was placed on paperwork. There was a lot of documentation with nothing to show for it. Contrary to this, the agile method places a huge emphasis on shortening the delivery time. Attention is placed on developing the product instead of just planning it.

Working Together

Principle number four states that stakeholders and developers work together closely during the development of the product or service. This principle pushes for a collaborative environment where individual members understand that they are working toward a common goal. If workers are based in remote locations, project managers should utilize the best tools to facilitate communication. Teams should work together to exchange ideas and understand each other. Through working together, increased productivity is achieved.

Working with a Group of Motivated People

Different people work toward achieving the purpose of the project. One of the main questions you should ask yourself as a project manager is, "Why did you hire them?" Certainly, you hired your team for their qualifications. This means that you should allow them to do what they do best. Don't micromanage. Micromanaging only sends the pool of talent packing. Working with the right team is vital. Consequently, you should have conducted thorough scrutiny beforehand. This means that you trust your team members to deliver.

Project managers or scrum masters should do their best to provide the support that the team needs. Also, they should regularly monitor what the team is doing to ensure that they are following the required guidelines. The significant thing here is that the team should gain the perception that you trust them to deliver.

Face-to-Face Communication

Simply stated, a project manager should strive to shorten the period for getting answers to their questions. Therefore, the face-to-face method of communication is regarded as an ideal form. The agile management method requires that people work together in an environment where they can easily hold face-to-face interactions. This doesn't mean that advanced methods of communication should not be used, however. Besides advocating for face-to-face interaction, the project manager should incorporate the use of advanced communication tools. If there are workers in distant locations, video calling is imperative. The point is to create a more collaborative communication environment.

Is the Product Working?

The primary metric to measure the success of

the project is whether the product works. If you are developing software, success is measured by whether the software is operational. Ideally, your success is not measured by checking off tasks; this is just part of the process. However, the success of the project is gauged by the product's functionality. In other words, the purpose of the project is not to go through the process from beginning to the end. If the product does not work, all your efforts don't matter. Other factors that led to the completion of the project are irrelevant if the end product does not work.

Sustainable Development

The main reason why short sprints of activities are highly recommended in the agile methodology is not just to help in making quick changes, but it also aids in keeping the team motivated. Often, people burnout when they handle similar activities for a long period. This is normal. To prevent this, the agile methodology advocates for short productive bursts. By working on a particular activity for a short period, it leads to increased productivity. The project manager should set the right pace to handle small activities. The project's team should feel satisfied with their achievements.

Continuous Improvement

A project manager should always ensure that the product they are working on is constantly improving. Whether you are working on some coding or anything more concrete, it is imperative to confirm that improvements are seen at every step or stage. The last thing that you should do is to come back later to fix things you experienced earlier. If you must fix issues, fix them now. The goal is not to come back and do some cleaning. Make necessary changes as you progress. This way, you save a lot of time while ensuring that the product is delivered punctually.

Simplicity is a Vital Element

Simplicity is the key to delivering a product within the shortest time possible. This means that your role as the project manager is to eliminate complexities. The team players should not waste their time comprehending the process. Make it simple for them to complete it in time. The good news is that the process can be made straightforward using the project management tools available at your disposal. So, as part of ensuring that a project is completed successfully, make sure that your team doesn't focus on what is not important. Remember to use management tools to automate the process.

Self-Organizing Teams

The best way of knowing whether your team is agile enough is by gauging whether they are self-directed. A great team should take direction without being pushed around. If you find that you are micromanaging the team, then this is a red flag. The individual teams that you work with should do what needs to be done. They should be there to handle issues and propose ideal solutions. A project manager should only step in when challenging issues arise or interfere when something is wrong that needs to be addressed fast. In normal situations, things should run smoothly. The credit will not go to the project manager but to the self-organized teams.

Inspect and Adapt

Inspection and adaptation is another vital principle which must be embraced in agile project management. Throughout the development process, the team should regularly stop and inspect what can be done to make things better. If anything needs tuning, this should be done right away. Making adjustments here and there is what guarantees that the project succeeds.

Adhering to the 12 principles of agile project management is vital to the success of any project. It doesn't matter which project you are working on, using these principles, you will realize that it is easy to deliver a product within a specified timeframe. Most importantly, you will reduce common productivity risks while effectively controlling the project's costs. Put simply; you will increase your chances of succeeding in your project management tasks.

Chapter 3: How to Apply the Agile Project Management Method Effectively

The importance of applying the agile project management method is to boost the chances of successful projects. In this case, the agility of your team ensures that the team is productive over an extended period. From the information discussed in the previous chapter, there are many benefits associated with the agile management method. On the surface, these benefits appear easy to attain. However, it is worth noting that not every project will benefit from using the agile project management method.

To ensure that you effectively apply agile to your project management, it is imperative to understand whether the method is right for you. Adopting the agile method means that your company will depart from how it used to work. Agility will demand a fast-paced way of doing things. Everything will have to be spelled out beforehand.

Accordingly, it is vital for your organization to determine whether or not it is up for the challenge. To find out, you need to answer the following questions:

- **Are you willing to initiate projects without knowing their outcome?**

By adopting the agile project management method, you will have to act fast. The method fosters the idea of moving quickly and constantly conducting tests during the product development process. This is not easy. It is stressful if not managed effectively. So, are you ready to take on the challenge?

Before adopting the agile method, reflect on whether you are prepared to put your product out there for testing before it's completed. It is essential to be prepared to test your cake before it is fully baked.

- **How risk-cautious are you?**

Adopting the agile method of project development implies that you will be taking on more risks as compared to the traditional way of doing things. While using this method, you must embrace the idea of learning from your mistakes as you strive to deliver a product that meets customers' requirements. Having said this, take a step back to evaluate whether you can handle risks. If you are going to take the agile route, you must be ready to deal with unknown issues or risks which could arise during product development.

- **Do you have an agile team?**

Determine whether your team is agile enough to handle the project's demands. Remember one of the principles of the agile method is that it pushes for a more collaborative environment. As such, your team should be ready to work together toward a common goal. The team members should set their differences aside and work harmoniously. Undeniably, if your team is not agile enough, then the agile project management method will not be as effective as it could be.

If you are satisfied with the answers to these questions, you are ready to change the way of doing things in your company. The following section will take you through a step-by-step process of applying the agile project management method to your company activities. Through the comprehensive guide provided in this section, you can learn how to develop your products in the agile way.

Step 1: Define Your Vision during a Strategy Meeting

The first thing that you need to address during the early stages of the agile project is your vision.

What does your project aim to solve? This is the bigger picture of whatever you wish to do. It gives your team a purpose and a mission. Product companies can best formulate their visions through the Elevator Pitch. This concept defines your target customer. Also, it should say something about the need that the project will address. Notably, it should also reflect on the main benefit of using the product set to be launched or introduced. In other words, what is the compelling reason which would motivate people to buy the product?

During this phase of the agile project, certain individuals should be present. Key stakeholders include managers, directors, and other executives, as well as the product owners.

When should you define your vision? Essentially, the meeting should occur before kicking off any project. If a project is underway, a strategy meeting could also be organized to guarantee that all members are informed about existing updates.

Step 2: Develop a Product Roadmap

After coming up with a vision, next is for the product owner to translate the vision into a roadmap. This is a visual summary which maps out the vision and the direction that the product development will take. It acts as a plan to be used in executing the strategy. Note that the roadmap uses a loose time frame. This means that the planning process does not simply focus on defining each step. Rather, the roadmap identifies and prioritizes the efforts required for delivering a usable product.

The best roadmap is goal-oriented one. Formulation of a roadmap should be carried out by the product owner, but input from other stakeholders should also be welcomed. For instance, the development, marketing, support, and sales representatives should be consulted. The process of creating a roadmap should be done right after the strategy meeting.

Step 3: Create a Release Plan

After developing a working strategy and a plan you will use to achieve your goals, the next step is to come up with a timetable. This is where the release plan comes in. During this stage, the product owner creates a high-level timetable which is utilized for the release of a working product. You should realize that agile projects will have several releases. Features must be prioritized to guarantee you can launch at any time.

The timetable will have to consider the complexity of the project and sprints length. All team members should be present during the release plan. It is during this step that you get the team members fired up and ready to take up the challenge which awaits them.

Step 4: Sprint Planning

The initial steps discussed here feature the macro view of the agile project development phase. The sprint planning step is a micro view, as it pays attention to the specific tasks that will be carried out to develop the product. Usually, an ideal sprint lasts from one to four weeks. The length of the sprint should be the same throughout the development process. The significance of having equal sprint length is that it allows the team members to effectively plan how future work will be handled based on past performance.

At the onset of the sprint cycle, the project manager and other team members must come up with a short list of backlog items to complete within the allocated sprint timeframe.

All team members must be present during the sprint planning step. Their contributions will make a huge difference in the development of a product which is tailored to the needs of customers.

Step 5: Holding Daily Meetings

Daily meetings work closely with the day to day sprints you create. The project manager will organize daily meetings where discussions about what was completed the previous day occur. It is during these meetings that any existing roadblocks are identified. Usually, the daily meeting lasts for about 15 minutes. In addition to discussing what was completed yesterday, the team also talks about what should be done today and the existing roadblocks preventing them from meeting set goals.

Every member of the team must understand the significance of holding regular meetings. Agile project management is all about swiftness. This can only be attained through regular monitoring of the project's progress. The daily meetings make it possible to identify areas that need improvement and work on matters which may be a stumbling block.

Step 6: Sprint Review

Assuming that everything goes as planned during the sprint cycles, your team should have a working product at this stage. If you are developing software, the software should be functioning once you get to this step. At this time, the team members should review what they have already done. The review process *should be attended by the stakeholders as they have to see the product working. Essentially, this is where you show off and tell more about the product.

The significance of this step is that all the team members get to sit together to determine whether the requirements were met in the development stages. The product owner can accept or reject some of the features which have been incorporated in the product. If there are errors, the team can discuss ways to deal with them in the next sprint. Agility is all about learning and correcting mistakes at each sprint cycle. It is worth pointing out that the sprint review should be conducted after every sprint. Hence, the team cannot take on another sprint without reviewing the first one.

Step 7: Sprint Retrospective

At this step, the team members discuss how the previous sprint went, and they also take time to discuss how the next sprint will be improved. The idea of agile project management is not just to plan. It also strives to ensure that a project's progress is well monitored and improved throughout the development process. The advantage gained is that changes can easily be made even in the late stages of development. Just like the sprint review, the sprint retrospective should be carried out after every sprint.

After this step, the product owner should have a functioning product. You can launch the product at any time and get feedback from your customers as you make changes. The continuous process of delivering a product without actually fully completing it is what makes the agile method powerful. You don't have to work on a product for the entire year and release it only to find out there are some core functionality aspects that are missing. This could be devastating, as you would have to start the entire process of product development again. The agile method helps you develop the product in sprints and monitor it until it meets the customer expectations.

Step 8: Make Mistakes and Improve

At the end of every sprint, you should gather feedback and find ideal ways to improve. Making mistakes should not be taken negatively. Rather, the group should learn from their mistakes and adjust accordingly. The sprint review and sprint retrospective steps should identify these mistakes. Afterward, the team works together to propose solutions to deal with mistakes.

Step 9: Mature

Regular inspection and learning from mistakes will assist the team in growing and maturing. They will learn a lot from past mistakes. Therefore, it will be easier for them to circumvent challenges in future projects, and there will be an improvement from one sprint exercise to the other.

Think about it this way: big companies such as Microsoft and Google can keep their products updated every week by using the agile method. This is why you find them reminding you of regular updates to their products. Put simply; their products develop with constant improvements tailored to meet the needs of the customer. They remain the best in the market because they use the agile project management method. Bear this in mind when you think about bringing agile to your team.

Chapter 4: Setting Up Your Own Agile Environment and the Team Composition

After understanding how to apply the agile method in your organization, it is imperative to comprehend how to set it. The environment where your team works in should be agile enough to guarantee that set goals are achieved. As mentioned previously, agility here refers to the swiftness of adapting to change by a company. The working environment should be conducive to support an agile workplace. This section will take you through the steps take to create an agile surrounding. We will also take a closer look at the composition of an agile team.

What is an Agile Environment?

What does it mean to work in an agile environment? This refers to an environment that creates and nurtures a culture to motivate a team of individuals to work in harmony toward a common goal. High value is placed on the interactions of these individuals and their skills.

An agile organization can be distinguished from another organization that uses traditional project management strategies. Some characteristics of agile organizations can help understand what an agile environment should be. Common traits of an agile environment are briefly discussed below.

Leadership is About Purpose

Agile environments strive to shorten the distance between developing a product and getting it to the hands of the end consumer. Consequently, leadership in an agile environment places a stronger emphasis on the purpose of the mission instead of other less important factors. In this case, the best leadership is defined by how the product reaches its consumers rather than the process.

Self-Organizing Teams

One of the most evident traits of an agile environment is that it is comprised of self-organizing teams. These are people who know what they are doing. As the project manager, select individuals who have the skills to meet the project demands. A self-organizing team works with minimal supervision since they believe that the project manager trusts their abilities.

Stable Team Membership

An agile team will also be stable over the long haul. With the support and motivation from their project manager, team members will find no reason to leave the organization. As such, an agile environment is comprised of stable team members who are ready and willing to support the organization in meeting its goals.

Face-to-Face Interaction

This is a reminder of one of the policies of an

agile project management methodology. In an agile environment, face-to-face interaction is advocated as the best form of communication. There might be other forms of communication used to ensure that interaction is facilitated regardless of geographic location. However, face-to-face interactions are valued over other forms of communication.

Full Transparency

One of the best things about an agile environment is that no one is kept in the dark. Keep in mind that individuals gain quick access to the project's progress through the task boards. Therefore, if anything needs changing, each member of the team can have a say on what needs to be altered. Such transparency in an agile environment instills trust. Team members are more motivated since the organization trusts them enough to share everything relating to the project.

Sprints

Sprints are at the heart of any agile project management method. This refers to a time-boxed period where the scrum team works to achieve a set amount of work. If your organization fails to work using sprints, then you are not working in an agile environment. The best way to gain agility in your organization is by working in sprints. By dividing the project into smaller projects, it is easy to make any changes which might be required. Also, one of the main reasons for using sprints is that it helps in ensuring that the end product meets customer requirements.

Continuous Improvement

Another trait of an agile environment is that it fosters a continuous environment throughout the project development process. When using agile, the main focus is not delivering a complete product after a particular period. Rather, the focus is placed on continuously improving a working product throughout its different development phases. Through continuous improvement, issues relating to the product can be identified and rectified. Also, the team improves products based on customer demands.

With these traits in mind, you should have a glimpse of what working in an agile environment should resemble. Your organization should embrace the culture where people get to work together toward a common goal. Also, working in sprints should be evident. Your team should work in short periods where they get an opportunity to evaluate their progress and make adjustments accordingly. Most importantly, your company should embrace the essence of continuous improvement as a way of meeting customer requirements. Ultimately, when all these traits are evident in your organization, you can be sure that you will be delivering quality products to customers.

For your organization to portray the qualities of an agile environment, there are several areas you should tackle.

Transforming to an Agile Mindset & Culture

The introduction of new technologies has transformed the way things work in most organizations. These technologies have pushed people to work in volatile environments where they have to adapt to changes fast. This mostly applies to the IT sector as systems can easily be considered obsolete quite quickly. To ensure that organizations keep up, teams have to be agile. They have to be flexible to adapt to fast changes occurring around them. This begins by transforming into an agile mindset. How do you create an agile mindset amongst your team members?

Embrace Flexibility

A key feature of the agile method is that people

should be flexible. For instance, when using a particular strategy to develop a product, the team members should be flexible to switch strategies at ant step of the development process.

Understand the Context

As the project manager, it is vital for you to understand the complexity of the working environment. If you are going to implement an agile method, you need first to understand whether the method is applicable or not. Indeed, most organizations strive to implement the agile method since it is the "in-thing." Since this is what other successful organizations are doing, most organizations conclude that they should do it, too.

Sure, the agile method is an ideal technique to use, but the project manager should be careful when implementing it. They should first understand the complexity of their environment beforehand.

Embodying the Agile Manifesto

For an organization to develop an agile culture, they first have to understand how to live by the values of the agile method. These values have been defined by the Agile Manifesto. They are different from the 12 principles which were discussed at the beginning of this manual. There are four values which are outlined in the Agile Manifesto.

- ### *Individuals and Interactions*

This is the first value of the Agile Manifesto. Here, interactions of people are valued over processes and tools. Ideally, it is people who work to respond to the needs of any business. Also, they are the ones who drive development in an organization. Therefore, they should be highly regarded as compared to processes and tools. In situations where development is achieved by heavily relying on processes and tools, then it is quite likely that the team will not be flexible to change. In the end, they will not meet consumer needs.

- ### *Software Over Documentation*

The idea of documenting any production process is what consumed a lot of time back then. This is what led to delays in the product development process for software development. The agile method reduces documentation by ensuring that more focus is placed on the product instead of the process.

- ### *Customer Collaboration*

The agile method stresses the importance of the customer being included in the project development process. Teams should seek consumer feedback regularly by offering them product demos.

- ### *Responding to Change*

Conventional software development teams tried

their best to avoid change because the change was considered an expense. Changing anything during the product development process meant that the team would have to begin the development process all over again. The agile method uses sprints to ensure that change can easily be adopted without necessarily changing the whole product development process. Using the agile method warrants that change constantly improves a product. There is an additional value placed on the product to ensure that customers are pleased with it.

Developing an agile mindset and culture requires that the team members memorize these values. This manifesto tells how people should behave in the organization. As the project manager, it is important to coach your team on the essence of knowing these values and abiding by them while they are working.

Transparency

Transparency is a fundamental quality that ensures that the agile method is applied successfully in your organization. Through transparency, agile culture is easily developed. People in your organization should build on the culture of openness on anything that hinders them from reaching set goals. The significance of transparency is that it opens doors for inspection and adaptation. If problems are identified, even during the late stages of the development process, they can be inspected and handled before a product is introduced to the customer. Everything in the organization should be open as this is a way in which a culture of openness in nurtured. Interestingly, some organizations make salaries and bonuses transparent. You simply need to find an ideal way to make your team members realize that it is important to be honest about everything about the project.

Be a Change Agent

Indeed, changing the mindset of people who have been used to a certain working methodology is not an easy job. Don't expect change to come overnight. You must be the change agent in your organization. As the project manager, your role is not just to remind your team about their duties. Rather, remind them about the agile values. Coach them about the best practices that lead to an agile environment. Doing this is the best way to develop an agile mindset and culture.

Talk with People

One killer move which can easily destroy the chances of your project team succeeding is talking about each other. If different teams are working toward a common goal, you should not talk to the management about how a particular department is functioning. Doing this only reduces trust, transparency, and the respect that the team once had. It destroys their morale. There is a good reason why sprint meetings are held daily. Take this opportunity to talk with them and not about them. If there are any issues with the team, identify them during sprint meetings. Remember, you need to foster transparency as a way of adopting an agile mindset and culture.

Creating an agile mindset and culture begins by ensuring that the project team understands the Agile Manifesto and knows the importance of adopting the values which have been outlined. Also, as the project manager, you should always remember to lead by example. Change begins with you. You must lead by showing other team members that you are agile. You need to prove to them that you are acting without any kind of secrecy. Ultimately, people will follow the right path toward adopting an agile mindset and culture.

How to Set Up an Agile Environment

The rapidly changing environments we exist in today have transformed industries. Organizations have stepped up their game, and they understand that they need to gain competitive advantage by keeping up with change. For instance, organizations gain a competitive advantage over their rivals by adopting the latest technology. It is an ability to change that makes firms agile and different from others in their industries of operation. An agile organization provides workers with the right environment they need to embrace speed and flexibility. To transform to a more agile organization, there are three key areas you need to address.

- People

- Structure

- Process

People

The best place to begin transforming your organization to become agile is the human resources department. Conventionally, companies have been used to hiring people based on their skills. This leads to a situation where human resources is limited to a particular skill set. When hiring people, they simply focus on whether they have the specific skills required.

To foster agility in your organization, it is imperative that you forgo a skills checklist. Focus on hiring a team that is not only collaborative but also creative. Find workers who are curious about trying new things to entice a customer. Through this approach, an organization creates a flexible and dynamic team. The good news is that a team assembled using this approach will easily adjust to changes that constantly occur during the product development process.

Structure

An agile environment in the workplace can be attained by getting rid of existing complexities, which tend to drag business processes at all levels. Doing away with these challenges will lead to better decisions being made.

The team's structure should also be carefully defined. In this case, the role of the project manager is not traditional. Conventional management strategies believed that the role of a manager was to assign tasks to other employees and ensure that they are done accordingly. In an agile workplace, this is not the duty of a manager. A manager's role is to communicate more about the goals and objectives, important metrics, and motivate the team working on the project. Do you notice the variation?

Adopting a traditional hierarchical structure only slows the way things are done in the organization. Therefore, it is vital that the right structure is adopted to guarantee that a stable and functional agile environment is achieved.

Process

Besides focusing on people and the structure of your organization, you can alter processes to gain an agile environment. Numerous companies have processes in place to ensure that a product is developed on time and delivered to consumers. Nonetheless, most of these companies face a huge challenge concerning their flexibility. In most cases, they are not flexible enough to adapt quickly to changes and market demands.

To push for an agile environment, organizations need to have processes which support collaboration, quick decision making, accountability, transparency of information, and so on. These are some of the attributes that should be evident in an agile organization.

Team Structures

For a project to be successful, the project manager has to bring together different people with varying skills. Their ability to work together for a common goal determines the success or failure of any project. There are many people and different roles who could be involved in an agile project team.

Product Owner

As the name suggests, this is the individual with expertise on the product and its requirements. The product owner works hand-in-hand with the development team to make sure that product requirements are considered at every stage of its development. A product owner could be identified as a customer representative.

Development Team Members

Simply put, these are the individuals who create the product. If you are developing software, for example, team members include programmers, designers, testers, data engineers, etc. You should note that the development team members will have varying skills. This is vital for the achievement of the project's goals.

Scrum Master

The scrum master works closely with the development team. This individual works to offer support to the development team by making sure that the agile process remains consistent throughout the process. Scrum masters are most effective when they have the power to push for changes without necessarily seeking permission.

Stakeholders

Stakeholders are individuals with interest in the project. They are not accountable for the product. However, they are there to provide the necessary input required. In the end, they are affected by the performance of the project. To guarantee that projects thrive, stakeholders should be included in the product development process and provide necessary support at every stage.

Agile Mentor

An agile method will be implemented successfully in an organization by relying on an agile mentor. This is an individual who has the first-hand experience with how the project method works. They are there to guide how to apply agile to the organization.

Essentially, the idea of creating an agile workplace all boils down to sticking to the Agile Manifesto. For an agile environment to be created in any organization, workers should first understand the core values and principles to follow. It is by following this manifesto that they will learn how to behave in an agile way.

Chapter 5: Tools for Quality Control in Agile Project Management

Managing projects is not an easy job. For that reason, there are several agile tools which help in dealing with the management challenge. A fundamental step in any management process is to ensure that product quality requirements are met. Therefore, as part of making sure that the agile method is implemented successfully, it is imperative to make use of quality control tools. There are several quality control tools which can be used, and some are discussed in this chapter.

Meeting quality demands when developing any product is always a major project constraint. To ensure that the quality of a product is up to par, there are three quality management processes to follow that include planning, performing quality assurance and quality control. Depending on the process, there are varying tools to use. However, some tools can be used interchangeably.

A closer look into the 12 principles of agile project management reveals that they promote the development of a quality product directly or indirectly. Before getting into detail about quality control tools, consider the striking difference between quality management in traditional approaches versus those on agile methods.

First, in traditional approaches, testing a product was handled in the last phase of the project development process. Most features were tested months or years after they had been created. In agile, testing is done every day. When conducting daily sprints, testing is done to make sure that requirements are met. Automated testing of products is conducted to ensure that the process is quick and efficient.

Equally, when problems are identified in the late stages of product development, it poses a huge risk to the process. Using the agile method guarantees that bugs can be identified early enough, so they do not pose a danger to the development process.

Keeping in mind that there are project deadlines which need to be met, traditional approaches often shorten the testing phase. As a result, this leads to defective products being released to the market. The agile method carries out testing regularly, ensuring that product quality requirements are met.

Notably, defects in products are costly when they are identified during the late stages of its development. This applies to traditional quality management approaches. Conversely, since problems are easily identified at any phase of the agile development process, solving these problems is not costly.

Now, when selecting the right agile tools, it is vital to have criteria to help make the right choice. This is why there are several tools out there. Picking just one is not the best way to find the best quality control tool. Features you should consider are task management, integrations, team collaboration, agile metrics, and reporting and analytics.

Clarizen

Undeniably, when working with certain projects, there are activities or processes which are repeatable. The idea of going all over these activities at each phase of product development is a waste of time. An automation tool is helpful in this case. Clarizen serves the purpose as it is an automation software solution. A business with several related activities can use this software to transform how they do business. The automation of services will speed up processes and lead to efficiency.

Clarizen helps with listing tasks, schedules, communications, docs and files, and reporting. During the project execution phase, the software ensures that every team member is on the same page. Each person working on the project is allowed to experience how their contribution helps the team.

Trello

Another agile tool that comes highly recommended is Trello. If you are new to the world of agile project management, then this is the right tool for you. Trello is regarded as one of the easiest project management tools available. The best part about this tool is that you get to see it in action without paying a dime. With its simplicity, there are specific features that are not available in the free version of the tool. Nonetheless, for the best functionality, one has to pay the full version.

GitScrum

GitScrum is a project management tool that will help any project manager succeed in using agile. This tool stands out from others due to some unique features it offers. For instance, it has a time-tracking tool which aids in logging hours. Additionally, it has bug tracking feature which also allows the user to pull out bug reports and check their statuses. Useful Scrum features found in the product include a project calendar, checklists, changelog, customizable workflows, sprint planning, and reporting tools such as burndown charts. With this tool, the project team can upload and share files and communicate via discussion forums, as well as remaining constantly updated through email notifications.

Jira

When searching for the best agile project management tools, you will likely find Jira since it is widely used. Initially, Jira was used for checking bugs and tracking issues. However, as time passed, it was designed to become a fully developed, agile tool. With this tool, task management, reporting, and team collaboration become relatively easy.

One of the main pros of using Jira is that it offers flexibility when dealing with unique workflows. As such, the user can customize the workflow and process to suit their project. Equally, it offers the advantage of integrations. Users can take advantage of the seven day trial period to gauge whether Jira works for them.

Taiga

Taiga is an open source project management tool that is simple and easy to use. More importantly, it is powerful. Its functionality is focused on Kanban and Scrum and that it can easily create backlogs with sprints, user stories, and epics. Taiga allows social management, which helps teams when they need to assist each other. Additionally, there are other team collaboration and task management components for users. Nonetheless, its weakness is in its integrations and reporting aspects.

Pivotal Tracker

Project development, which follows the Kanban style, is best managed using Pivotal Tracker. This tool is appropriate for task management. With well laid out workspaces, multiple projects can easily be managed. The workspaces are also arranged in a way that a user easily identifies their priorities. There are also great analytic tools which aid in better understanding the project's health. Reporting using this tool provides a quick snapshot of how the project is performing. Besides these amazing features, the tool also takes integrations seriously. As such, you will find helpful integrations such as Slack, Zendeck, and GitHub. Smaller teams of less than three people can use this tool for free. However, larger teams will have to pay for the features that Pivotal Tracker offers.

Nostromo

Individuals working on digital projects will

benefit from the all-in-one Nostromo. Ideal features, including time administration, task management, reporting, analytics, and to-do lists. Since it is a new project management tool on the market, there are few integrations provided.

Hansoft

Hansoft is an ideal choice for many due to its adaptability. Organizations which tend to scale quickly should use this agile project management tool. There are also an array of learning tools provided with the package that include courses and webinars.

In terms of backlog management, Hansoft exceeds expectations. Users can easily group items based on themes, sprints, and epics. Also, items can be prioritized before assigning them to a particular sprint. The prioritized view of items helps users effectively work on the most pressing issues first.

Similarly, there are intuitive dashboards to provide all the team members with the insights they need throughout the project development process. This confirms that better and improved decisions relating to the project are made.

Blossom

Distributed teams can take advantage of the Blossom project management tool. Its customizable workflow shows the status of the project. Blossom facilitates the easy addition of comments, files, to-do lists, and more. The easy-to-use interface is uncomplicated and allows the team to see activities on the project.

Likewise, there are performance analytic tools which help to gauge how a project is performing right from its inception to delivery of the final product. Blossom is also good with integrations.

Ravetree

Ravetree is yet another good project

management tool. Unlike other tools, Ravetree is not limited to use by software teams. Any agile organization can utilize the unique features that include resource planning, time tracking, expense tracking, CRM, and digital asset management. Ravetree has a highly intuitive interface, which makes it easy for the team members to find the information they need.

This list is just a summary of some of the best agile project management tools available. There are varying features which make these tools stand out from each other. Therefore, it is important for you to go over the features and determine whether it is the best agile tool for you. The trial period could be a great way of testing the product without actually paying for it. Don't overlook the significance of the trial periods provided.

Managing Risk in Agile Project Management

When working with projects, managers and product owners often understand that there are risks in working on the project. Anything can happen when developing a product to be introduced to the market. Customers could either accept or reject the products, or the product being introduced could succeed or fail.

The notion of risk-taking implies that there are possibilities that failure could occur in the process. It is for this reason that the term risk-taking is used. Otherwise, it would have been called sure-thing-taking. Risks, therefore, are influential factors which would hurt the outcome of a project. Risk occurs through uncertainty. Project managers strive their best to deliver a quality product in spite of the many uncertainties which they cx face. Risk analysis allows a team working on a project to understand the likely uncertainties they could face.

Risk management is the plan that the team formulates to mitigate effects that could pose a risk to the success of a project. Things can easily go wrong when handling projects. It doesn't matter if you are working on a small or a big project; sometimes things go wrong. It is vital to ensure that there is a plan to minimize the possible impact when unpredictable events occur. What follows is a look into how managing risk in an agile environment should take place.

Step 1: Identify

The first step is to identify the dimensions of risk. There are two aspects in which risk could take. It could either be helpful or harmful or internal or external. There could be a SWOT analysis which could help in comprehending how risks affect the project. For example, if the risk is helpful, this could be regarded as a strength or an opportunity. On the other hand, if the risk is harmful, then it could be a major weakness or a threat.

The idea of managing risks primarily focuses on what is harmful. In this case, some of the major weaknesses that a project could suffer from include insufficient resources, an aggressive timeline, limited budget, technological uncertainties, lack of essential skills in the team, etc. Threats that could be faced include pandemics, economic uncertainty, trade tariffs, changing legislation, and geopolitical tensions. A closer look into threats and weaknesses unveils that weaknesses are things that can be controlled, whereas threats are those that cannot be easily controlled. While people may not have control over issues such as sickness, there are actions which can be taken to reduce the risk effects on projects.

Step 2: Classify

Once risks have been identified, the next thing is to classify them. The classification should be done based on the areas which are affected. Grouping should be done according to the likelihood of the risk. Likewise, the level of impact will also be an important consideration when classifying the risks which have been identified.

Step 3: Quantify

After classifying risks based on the extent of impact, likelihood of occurrence, or on areas which are impacted, the next thing is to quantify them. This is where you measure the impact of the risk or the likely impact of the risk if it occurs. Certainly, a risk assessment must be handled by an expert. For instance, if security systems are being assessed, this is something that the project manager cannot handle unless they are qualified in that area. The same case applies to other aspects which will have to be assessed, including quality, performance, and privacy.

Bearing in mind that an agile environment advocates for transparency, the team must sit together and discuss the assessment results. This will help a lot in bringing amicable solutions to the table.

Quantifying risks can be done using impact and probability. The impact of risk will measure the effect that it has on a project. Here, the impact could range from minimal to extreme. Minimal impact means that there is little influence that a particular risk could have on the project.

However, it doesn't mean that the risk should be ignored. Instead, the risk should be reviewed regularly to confirm that it is well mitigated. Impact classified as extreme means that it could result in project failure. Also, the extreme impact hurts the budget and timeline of the project. In worse cases, such risks could endanger the entire organization.

With regards to probability, the occurrence of risk could be quantified as very unlikely to occur to very likely to occur. If the risk could easily occur, then it could be classified as likely to occur or very likely to occur. Conversely, if there are minimal chances that it could happen, then it could be ranked as unlikely to occur or very unlikely to occur.

Step 4: Plan

To this point, you have identified and classified potential risks which could occur when handling any project in the organization. So, what should be done about these risks? Risk planning comes into play. You need to come up with a simple approach to use to deal with these risks. The plan should identify the actions which will be used to effectively manage risks. For instance, when dealing with risks with minimal impact on the project, ideal actions would be to review the risks quarterly. Also, it should be specified that no explicit actions are required since the risks pose no harm.

On the other hand, critical risks require urgent attention. Your plan should also explicitly point out that a responsible executive should be informed about it. A critical risk must be tracked daily to ensure that its effects are reduced considerably. Depending on how risks have been classified, your plan should clearly state the necessary action to be taken. In an agile environment, the risk plan should be accessible by all members working on a project. This helps in making sure that the team knows what actions should be taken contingent on the level of risk being faced.

As part of ensuring that risks are continuously managed, it is important to have a risk register. This is a register where records of the risks and their mitigation strategies are jotted down. The importance of this register is that it shows how a particular risk has changed since it was identified. If the risk was critical, the management strategies which have been used should make sure that the risk moves to the minimal category. This way, everyone is assured that risks have been effectively handled.

Step 5: Act

The last step you need to take while managing risks is to act. Essentially, you implement what has been stated in the risk mitigation strategies. However, the process is not as easy as it sounds. Often, people are accustomed to putting off things to a later date. Doing this renders the risk management useless. Risks should be dealt with as soon as they are identified. Remember, working in an agile environment means that you need to act swiftly.

Step 6: Repeat

The process of managing risks in an agile environment means that you have to repeat the process over and over again. It is a vicious circle to make sure that your project succeeds. It is important to note that the risk plan being used should be reviewed regularly to guarantee that ideal measures are used to mitigate potential risks.

Managing risks will always be a part of any project. Bearing in mind that numerous uncertainties could come up, it is essential to have a risk management strategy. The steps outlined here should help you in initiating a practical plan to manage risks. Note that a risk management strategy that works for another organization will not necessarily work for you. Different companies face different risks, whether they are developing similar products or not.

Chapter 6: The Main Benefits of Applying the Agile Method

At the beginning of this manual, we discussed several advantages of using the agile project management method. This section dives in further to look at the major benefits gained by organizations when they choose to use the agile method. In other words, we will look into some of the main reasons why the agile method is so compelling.

Quick Identification of Incorrect Approaches

Obviously, in a more traditional project management method, when a wrong path is used, it means that the entire project development process is probably in danger. In extreme cases, the entire project development process would have to be abandoned. This could cost the organization a lot of money as a product cannot be introduced to the market if it doesn't meet consumer requirements.

Using the agile method advocates for the fail-fast strategy. This is an approach whereby the product developers aim at getting fast feedback from customers or end users. After getting a response, changes are rapidly made to ensure that the product meets customer demands in every way.

Considering that there are numerous uncertainties to deal with, it is less expensive to quickly introduce a product to the market and learn whether it works or not. If the product is not functional, then it can be abandoned right away without spending any extra money, hence the term "fail-fast." Using the agile concept makes it easy to quickly identify use of any incorrect approaches. Ultimately, an organization will save a lot of time and money that would have been wasted on trying to introduce a product that does not meet the market demand.

Quick Decision Making

An agile environment brings together individuals in an organization to realize that their joined efforts help to realize project goals that have been set. Quick decisions can be made in daily meetings. Team members are fully aware that the agile method demands that face-to-face interactions are highly valued.

Collaborations Lead to Numerous Benefits

The idea of working in a collaborative environment has benefits for the entire organization. In this case, by people working together toward a common goal, they also have a shared desire to succeed. People and technological resources get to interact together to meet the project's goals fast. With the speedily changing environment, using agile tools comes in handy. These tools aid in ensuring that there is efficiency in the way of doing things. For instance, if there are repeated processes, agile tools conveniently confirm that such processes are automated. People, on the other hand, collaborate to solve new and existing issues which could hinder the success of any project.

Through collaboration, there are many project benefits.

1. The need for frequent changes arising from poorly clarified requirements is reduced considerably. Since team members work together transparently, they can clearly define the product requirements. Therefore, this reduces the need to go back and forth when these requirements have not been fully met.

2. Collaboration also helps a lot in terms of risk identification. Risks are quickly identified, and therefore, they are

handled efficiently.

3. A team that works together in harmony can easily realize their true potential because they can identify their strengths and weaknesses. The team can work toward exploiting these strengths while doing their best to deal with their weaknesses.

4. Collaboration also guarantees that continuous improvement is maintained throughout the product development process.

5. As collaboration improves in the organization, this also bears a positive impact on the organization. They will be able to adapt to sudden changes easily. In other words, the organization will be more agile when working with a collaborative team.

Change is Embraced

Working in an agile environment also fosters the quick adaptability to change. During the product development process, the importance of adapting quickly to change is a fact that the agile method promotes. Ideally, the push for change is one of the core values of the agile method. Therefore, as teams learn to make changes more often, they develop a culture where change is embraced regardless of the development stage. In this case, people understand that change leads to an improved product being delivered to consumers.

A Final Product with Useful Features

The best thing about using the agile method is that the product constantly goes through an evolution. Usually, a demo product is introduced to the market to seek consumer feedback, so customers contribute a lot to the development process. When the product is finally released to the market, it will have all the features that a customer would want. The likelihood of the product succeeding in the market is high because it features all the attributes a customer wants. Getting attention from the market is not challenging.

A Suitable Environment for Millennials

Millennials are the next generation to take over the many working positions occupied by baby boomers. The good news is that the fast-paced environment is what the millennials like. Agility at work will, therefore, favor millennials working in numerous organizations. Accordingly, creating an agile environment guarantees that workers feel motivated to work toward meeting business goals.

Delivering the Right Product

Above anything else, a huge benefit of using the agile method is that the right product is delivered to consumers. Since a product is carefully reviewed daily in each sprint meeting, any defects are easily identified early. Also, regular checking ensures that the product's requirements are met. If anything is not right, this can quickly be changed at any stage of the development process. The end product is close to perfection as the customer is provided with a product that has all the features it is expected to have.

An Exciting Environment to Work

An agile environment is an environment which promotes active involvement, cooperation, and collaboration among team members. This is an experience which excites many as they get to share tasks. Also, through such collaboration, the team helps one other overcome their weaknesses. Therefore, it is not just the organization that gets to benefit from the agile method but also the employees interacting with it. This leaves workers motivated every time they work on a project. Undeniably, such positive attitude amongst workers transforms into increased productivity at work.

Focus on Business Value

One of the main core values of the agile method is that it places a high value on people and interactions over processes and tools. Consequently, the agile method sees to it that stakeholders are more engaged in the development process. This assists in guaranteeing that the team understands the mission and vision of the organization. The team will focus more on the most important tasks during the product development process. They put a strong emphasis on their cooperation and collaboration, which leads to a high-quality product being introduced to the market at the right time and within the budget range.

Transparency

The agile method is all about transparency. Everything linked to the project is always discussed openly with interested parties and the development team. Since customers are also involved in the process, this helps to prioritize features and deal with bugs. Nonetheless, it is important for developers to inform customers that they are using demo products and not real products. Clearing the air prevents confusion and leads to reliable feedback data from customers.

Customized Team Structures

The notion of self-management creates a working environment where teams get to make decisions on their own. An agile workplace creates opportunities for workers to customize their job duties. This means that they can choose to work by following rules that suit them. Customization of team structures could take any direction. A group can organize itself based on work styles. Another team could organize itself according to their respective skills. Such customization creates a friendly workplace where individuals are highly motivated to work.

Improved Project Predictability

Using the agile project management method also aids a team to forecast how the project will progress. Improved predictability can be gained by making sure that sprint lengths are always the same. Additionally, task allocation should not be changed throughout the development process. With these practices in place, it makes it easy to predict the progress or the outcome of a project.

Higher Team Morale

Individuals who enjoy what they are doing are motivated to work without being pushed around. Working around a self-managing team paves the way for creativity and innovativeness. The exciting thing is that the respective groups will focus on sustainability. Consequently, this prevents team members from getting stressed over work-related issues. Don't forget that a supportive environment will also have a positive impact on how people work.

There are many reasons why the agile method is so wonderful. Using the agile project management method increases the chances of a product succeeding in the market. Equally, with the collaborative environment that team members work under, they adopt a culture where the need for change drives them. Overall, this benefits the organization both in the short and long-run. So, are you still hesitant whether you should use the agile project management method? Well, considering the discussed benefits, rest assured that there is more to gain when using this method to manage projects.

Chapter 7: Common Challenges in Using the Agile Method

Following the benefits of the agile method, it's a wonder that most organizations don't use it. Most organizations that do use it also don't succeed as expected. Using the agile project management method doesn't guarantee that a project automatically succeeds. There are common challenges which are faced by those implementing the agile method. This chapter will take a look at these challenges and discuss solutions. Knowing these challenges helps to understand the factors that hinder success. Users can adjust accordingly by avoiding regular pitfalls.

Refusal to Accept Change

One of the main challenges facing organizations trying to implement the agile method of project management is their unwillingness to accept change. People find it difficult to change the cultures to which they have been accustomed. Project managers find it a huge challenge to enforce an agile framework. To warrant that the agile method is successfully adopted, it is necessary for the organization to understand the importance of embracing new ideas. It is essential to note that once senior executives acknowledge the value of change, they will lead by example to push for a successful implementation of the agile method.

Distributed Team

Implementing the agile method also becomes a challenge when the team working on a project is not located in the same place. The success of the project is affected by geographic boundaries. People in different time zones sometimes have a hard time working together. Hence, collaboration is difficult to achieve. Ineffective communication influenced by the distributed team members will lead to dwindling productivity.

Changing Team Membership

The progress which had been initially achieved could all fade away if the team membership keeps changing. Truly, it takes time for the team to recover the time lost when team members change. If this keeps occurring, it means that the team is unstable. This also affects the team's morale as they feel wasted when they must repeat tasks. To ensure that a team gains stability, it is vital for the project manager to put together a team that will work together over the long haul. Of course, some circumstances might force team members to leave. However, such occurrences should be reduced by keeping individuals motivated.

Self-Organization

Still, about changing team membership, this creates a huge challenge for self-organization. It is daunting for team members to manage tasks on their own when people keep leaving. Besides, self-organization is not easy to achieve anyway. It doesn't come automatically after putting together a group of skilled individuals. A project manager should regularly coach the team and keep reminding them about the agile principles and core values. All these require time, which poses a huge challenge to most companies.

Absence of Skilled Product Owners

The agile project management method is new to most business analysts and stakeholders. This makes it difficult for them to give up their traditional way of doing things. To some extent, some of them think that the transparency that the agile method promotes prevents them from fully controlling how things are done. What they forget is that the agile method does not require stakeholders to keep pushing people around. Instead, self-organizing teams are there to ensure that tasks are handled with minimal supervision. Consequently, the absence of skilled product owners makes it challenging to fully adopt the agile method.

Tactical Issues

Using the agile project management method demands that users are provided with the necessary quality and risk management tools. These tools aid in promoting efficiency at work. If these tools are not provided by the organization, it is difficult to achieve the level of agility that the organization expects.

Unfamiliarity with Techniques

The adoption of the agile method means that different departments must be trained on how to implement the strategies in their routine activities and how to use these tools. The process could take a lot of time, which often discourages organizations from adopting the management method in the first place.

Considering these challenges, realize that agile is not as easy as it sounds. It is a process that looks simple on paper. However, the implementation process is another thing altogether. This is where most people fail. Teams working on a project cannot just read a book and adopt an agile culture. It doesn't work that way. It takes a lot of time to create an agile environment and nurture an agile culture in the organization. Keep in mind that you will be pushing for a change to an organization which has been using a traditional approach for decades. Therefore, you need to be patient and focused when implementing the agile method.

How Agile Can Easily Fail

It is also crucial for you to learn a thing or two about how you can fail when using the agile approach. There is no agile technique where the goal is a failure. However, poor planning by an informed team can easily lead to defeat. You might be using the best agile method, but it will not work if you do not use the right approach. The following lines will discuss how things can go wrong with the agile strategy. This information will provide you with the insight you need to avoid common pitfalls, which could hinder your organization from succeeding.

Planning Chaotically

A common myth surrounding the use of the agile method is that planning is not important. This is not true. In spite of having an agile system in place, it doesn't mean that planning is not important. Planning is the best way to execute your strategy. Fortunately, there is a tool to help your team plan effectively align their actions to the business goals. This tool is called the Agile Release Train, and it can help a company to plan projects even twelve months in advance.

Forming an Unstable Team

A lot has been said about collaboration. The success of any agile program depends on how well your team can combine their efforts. If you work with a team of individuals who understand each other, then you will have the upper hand. On the contrary, if your team is made up of strangers, it will be daunting for you to achieve the success you are looking to achieve.

Teams should be optimized to aid in reducing dependencies. An ideal group must be comprised of individuals who understand their job specifications. They should not wait for the project manager to guide them constantly. The best agile teams are made up of generalists. These are experts who will not depend on other specialty groups to complete their tasks.

Communicating Infrequently

Agile teams with poor communication will fail

quickly. The flow of communication in an agile environment should be continual. Regular interaction should be maintained with stakeholders who have an interest in the end product. The project manager should work to make sure that all members of the organization converse on similar wavelengths. It is quite likely that there will be certain terminologies that will be used in the workplace. A good team should have a uniform vocabulary concerning the product.

Poor Testing of Products

Having regular tests guarantees that quality is maintained when developing products. Poor testing is the fast road to failure. It is crucial for developers to accurately test products to make sure that they are up to standards. Regular tests aid in guaranteeing that the team finds it comfortable to adjust to changes.

Failing to Comprehend the Project's Scope

To ensure that the agile management approach functions optimally, it is crucial for the project manager to create a roadmap. This roadmap guides the development team on how tasks will be carried out. It lays the path to be taken to ascertain that a functional product is obtained at the end of each sprint. Therefore, it is important that all members of the team understand the project's scope from the start. This ensures that every step is in line with the project's goals.

Disregarding Customer Feedback

Customer feedback is what will bring about changes in the agile system. Failure to heed to consumer evaluation only leads to frustration. Your team will be disappointed that in spite of their efforts, they did not succeed. Customer comments should be highly regarded as they warrant that product requirements are fully met. Absence of customer feedback makes it a daunting task to know how to prioritize. Ultimately, the development team might end up disregarding what is most important in the eyes of the customer.

Chapter 8: Tips and Tricks to Make Your Agile Project Management System Efficient

Undeniably, different teams could use the agile project management method and obtain varying results. Some will succeed in using the agile method, whereas others could fail. The point here is that how the agile method is implemented makes a huge difference in the success or failure of a project. This chapter delves in to discuss some of the tips which could help in ensuring that the agile project management system is efficient.

Using Time Management Techniques

One of the most important things to consider when working with an agile team is time management. As a project manager, it is imperative that people manage their time effectively, as they would be handling a wide array of tasks in the organization. Therefore, it is vital for the project manager to take care of all these tasks at once while ensuring that quick turnaround time is maintained.

To help you plan your day, make use of agile tools to assist you in keeping track of what needs to be done. Agile tools will conveniently schedule pending tasks which need to be completed by you and your team.

In situations where you are not tech savvy, you can use a simple to-do list. This list will act as a reminder of what needs to be done at a specific time. Confirm that important tasks are prioritized over others. As the project manager, making the best use of your time will help to ensure that scheduled tasks are not delayed. In the end, projects will be handled in time without skipping the requirements.

Point Out the Project Requirements

The success of a project is determined by the

outcome. This implies that the end product after completion of the project defines whether the project was a success or not. In line with this, the project's success is evaluated by considering whether the product features all the requirements that consumers expect. Therefore, for a project to succeed, pointing out the project requirements is necessary. This is a fundamental step which guarantees that the development team understands what needs to be done. The project manager should coordinate tasks which lead to the achievement of the project requirements. Ideally, this is what matters most.

Hiring a Qualified Project Manager

The agile project management system will not function optimally without a qualified project manager. This person who has sufficient experience will understand what needs doing for a particular project to succeed. Equally, a credible manager will know how to allocate tasks to different individuals based on their qualifications. More importantly, they will find a way to make sure that the process is not only productive but also exciting at the same time.

When things go wrong in the project development process, an ideal manager steps in and proposes amicable solutions. The best part is that they also know how to win trust from clients through effective communication. Therefore, a qualified project manager gets the information they need from trusted clients on what needs to be changed on a product to meet consumer needs. Indeed, there are many reasons why hiring the right manager should be prioritized as they are the overall drivers of the project — choosing the wrong individual for the job will only risk project failure.

Providing Frequent Updates and Demos

The best way for an agile project to be efficient is by maintaining regular communication with regards to the project's progress. This infers that both the stakeholders and clients need to stay up-to-date with how the product is coming along. Moreover, a project manager needs to communicate with them about their duties. They need to be aware that their contribution assists in making the project a success.

When the project is underway, they need to constant updating about the product's functionality and deadlines. If there are any issues with the product, this information should also reach them. Effective communication confirms that the project is progressing smoothly with minimal hitches.

Additionally, stakeholders and customers should be provided with demos while the product is still "in the kitchen." Don't wait until your cake is fully baked to present it to them. This could be risky to your organization in case changes need to be made. Consequently, it is prudent to offer demos as a way of evaluating consumer reaction toward the product even before it gets to the market. Remember the aspect of "failing fast?" It will save you a lot of money if the product is not what the consumers want. Quick changes to the product can also be made without negatively affecting your organization's performance.

Regular Communication with Your Team

There are many benefits to making sure that regular communication is delivered to your team. Undeniably, communicating more often prevents misunderstandings from occurring. If there are any unclear requirements that the team fails to understand, this can also be ironed out through regular communication. By making sure that your team is informed about each step that they take, this increases the likelihood of project success.

Defining Critical Milestones

The success of a project is largely dependent on the main phases which need serious attention.

As the project manager, you must make sure that these phases are identified as the project continues. The team members must understand that certain phases are more important than others. To guarantee that the stages are successful, it is vital for the project manager to evaluate after each stage ends. Before proceeding to the next stage, the project manager should confirm that the project requirements have been fully met. Ultimately, when all the milestones are put together, there is a high probability that the project will succeed. Defining critical milestones acts as indicators that the team is doing its best to meet the project's goals.

Anticipating Project Setbacks

In spite of your well-laid-out plan, you should always expect that something can go wrong. It doesn't matter whether you hired the best project manager in town or not. Anything could happen to your project. How you deal with the challenges you face will have a huge impact on the overall performance of the project. To be on the safe side, pay attention to warning signs. Check whether there are missed deadlines, listen to complaints from stakeholders and any other signs which could indicate there are problems with the project. Dealing with these issues ensures that you get back on track and deliver a quality product in time.

Note that preventing a crisis from happening keeps your project on track. Moreover, your team will be confident that the project is progressing just as expected. So, it is vital for any project manager to anticipate setbacks and learn how to deal with them effectively.

Sadly, not all challenges or crises can be mitigated. There are some obstacles which could threaten to burn down the whole project. Still, in such instances, crisis management skills come in handy. Project managers should learn how to deal with situations they least expect. They should be flexible to changes and confident that they can make fast decisions when operating in an agile environment.

Project Evaluation

Another tip which guarantees your agile project thrives is through evaluation. Every project you handle should be considered a learning tool. A good manager takes the time to review how the project performed. All the components of the project should be evaluated to determine whether some areas could be improved in the next projects. By learning from past performance, a project manager can find ideal ways of improving in the future.

Transition Support

Implementing the agile method in your organization will not be an easy task. There is a lot that needs to be done to embrace the agile culture. This calls for good coaching, which will ensure that people understand the benefits that can be achieved by adopting the agile method. Coaching should be there to provide support when mistakes are made. Truly, you shouldn't expect your team to be perfect right after introducing the agile method. Give them time to adjust.

Support should also be provided in the form of mentoring in specific roles. Some members of the team might be faster in understanding the method better than others. This doesn't mean that you should allow others to drag behind. As the project manager, work to empower each person and ensure that they are in line with other members. This is what brings about stability in your development team. Ultimately, you will increase the likelihood of a successful project.

Total Openness and Transparency

Once you implement the agile method in your

organization, nothing needs hiding. You cannot mask how people are doing things. You cannot hide the progress of the project. The poor quality of your product cannot hide since you will be testing it with the consumers. There is nothing hidden in an agile environment. This is how your optimal agile environment should look. The agile tools you use should help you in maximizing on the quality of output. Total openness and transparency guarantee that you solve existing challenges, which might be evident in the project development process. Accordingly, it all begins with you setting the perfect example by being open and transparent in how you engage with your team.

Early Feedback

An agile system will also succeed if the team works to find a way of putting the product being developed in front of the consumers. As the product develops, consumers should test its demo product. They should know how it is functioning. This way, the team gets early feedback and can make changes where necessary. Getting early feedback warrants that the team can easily adapt to changes. The best part is that early feedback also helps in making sure that the right product is delivered to the customer. It reduces the risk of speculation. Knowing what the customer wants and working toward meeting their demands will increase the chances of project success.

Value over Activity

The notion of working in an agile environment might be confusing to many. Yes, agility requires that rapid changes should be adopted in any process. However, to succeed in your agile system, your team needs to embrace value over activity. Their focus should not just be to get things done. Rather, a higher emphasis should be on creating value. To ensure that this point sinks in, your team should go over the core values outlined in the Agile Manifesto.

Shared Accountability

Your agile system will blossom if you develop a culture where no one gets blamed for their part. The team working on a project should value the importance of shared accountability. All team members should be accountable for the outcome of the project. This means that if anything goes wrong, the entire team is at fault. This way, individuals understand the importance of collaborating for a common goal. Working together is what leads to increased productivity. Thus, this is what should be advocated for by the project manager.

A closer look at tips and tricks reveals the values and principles that the Agile Manifesto promotes. Indeed, for any agile system to succeed in the long-run, people and interactions should be valued over processes or tools. It is how people interact with each other that will contribute to the success of a project. Project developers are the persons who will respond to consumer requirements; so this is a value which needs upholding.

Equally, consumers should be involved in the product development process. This helps to ensure that their expectations are met and are achieved by providing them with product demos at each step of the development process. Doing this provides the development team with insights on what needs to be done to make sure that a product is what the customer needs.

Remember that agility is also more about responding to change. The advent of the internet has transformed how corporations behave in their respective industries. Today, these corporations exist in volatile environments, and to keep up, they must embrace change. Without transition, customers will turn to rival products as they meet their ever-changing demands. So, for an agile system to function successfully, change is inevitable.

Chapter 9: Key Metrics to Measure Agile Success

So, after successfully implementing your agile method, you will want to find out whether it succeeded or not. How will you know whether the agile system made a difference? The chances are that you are thinking about the product quality since the agile method promotes the idea of focusing on the product and not the process. Well, you should understand that there is more to succeeding in agile than just delivering a quality product. This chapter will help you understand the key metrics to help you in gauging the level of success of your agile system.

Before gauging the success of agile, there are several questions you need to ask yourself.

- **Does the organization have an agile culture?**

The success of your organization will be

determined by its agile maturity. All the departments in your organization should portray some level of maturity since the agile system developed. How processes are handled will also tell a lot about how the agile culture has transformed your team. For instance, if you notice that sprint meetings are conducted daily, then it will mean that your team has transformed. Since you are aware of the agile values, actions of your team should be in line with these values.

- **Is the organization credible?**

Additionally, you should also strive to find out whether your team is delivering the product that was promised to the customer. This is a straightforward process as you only need to confirm whether the requirements of the end product have been met. An agile system that helps the team meet customer demands can be identified as a good system. With time, your company will gain the credibility it seeks since it will be producing top quality products.

- **Does the organization meet its commitments?**

It is also crucial for the project manager to consider whether the organization meets its commitments by using the agile technique. Its commitments here relate to the product features and meeting project deadlines. Equally, the company should be delivering the product in time just as the clients were promised. The velocity of a team will have a huge influence with regards to the group meeting its obligations. The collusive efforts of the entire team should complete an array of tasks within a specified period.

- **Does the organization produce quality products?**

Getting answers to this question will unveil the performance level of the company. If the team produces quality products, then it implies they are performing well. On the contrary, defective products mean that something is not right with the agile system being used.

The following are essential metrics which will aid you in measuring the success of your agile system.

On-Time Delivery

One key metric which will help you measure the success of your agile initiative is on-time delivery of the product. By meeting the expectations of customers, you can gauge the level of success. A product that hits the market at the right time gains a competitive edge over rivals in the market. People will want to use products that get to the market first.

If the product meets its requirements, there is a good chance that they will stick to that product in the long run. Measuring the success of an agile initiative through on-time delivery is done through the burnup charts. These are tools which help project managers to track the progress of a project. These charts provide the development team with the information they need to predict the completion dates. The charts also help them to ensure the process is on schedule.

Product Quality

Equally, product quality tells a lot about the agile method. The quality of the product will influence the success of the project in several ways. First, it will have a huge impact on customer satisfaction. A product that satisfies the needs of the customers performs well in the market. It means that the project was carried out successfully. Also, a project is successful since the revenue gained from the sale of the product meets the organization's goals. So, in many ways, the product quality tells a lot about how the organization performed.

Customer Satisfaction

The success of your agile system can also be gauged through customer satisfaction. Here, you will have to consider the sales figures. If the product is selling in the market, this is a clear sign that you performed well. Your efforts in delivering a good product will pay off. You could also consider the number of calls you get concerning the product. If many calls are asking for details, then it means that your project performed well. Simply put, customers will be happy with what you delivered, and therefore, your returns on investment will be high.

Business Value

The overall business value gained through the use of the agile method is also used to measure how good your agile system is. It is important to remind you that this is what the Agile Manifesto promotes. The business value is highly regarded above anything else. The value to the business is gained when contract requirements are met or delivering a product at the right time.

Product Scope

You can also measure the success of your agile initiative by looking at the product scope. At the beginning of the development process, you set goals regarding the features and requirements that you need to put into a particular product. At the end of the process, meeting these goals is truly rewarding. As such, knowing that the product delivered to the market has all the requirements the product owner expected, is a sign that the project is a success. It is a clear indication that the agile method worked.

Project Visibility

The level of success of your agile method can also be defined by its visibility. The best agile system is one where everything is open for the entire team to see. Knowing that all members with interest in the project are aware of its progress is a way of determining its success. It wouldn't be successful if things were not laid out in the open.

Process Improvement

It is also possible to measure how your agile system is performing through process improvement. One of the main reasons why the agile method leads to an overall enhancement in product quality is the notion of continuous improvement. The frequent changes made after every sprint will, in the end, determine the quality of the product. If there is a steady improvement of the product at every stage, it means that the end product features what the customer expects. So, your agile method should constantly make things better in the project development process.

Satisfaction Surveys

The highest priority of any agile program is to meet the needs of the customer. One way of finding out whether this goal is being achieved is through satisfaction surveys. Customers can use demo products and help in knowing whether their demands are being met. Also, satisfaction surveys can be filled by team members. In this case, members answer questions relating to their experience working with the organization. Such team surveys identify existing loopholes in the product development group.

Defects

Defects will always be a part of any project. Regardless of how skilled the development team is, there will be errors in the product development process. Any good team should work to make sure that they minimize flaws. The idea of tracking mistakes also assists in measuring the performance of the agile program. The team working on creating a new product will know how well they are doing to prevent defects in the development process.

Project managers want to know how their agile initiatives perform. Therefore, it is imperative for them to consider the metrics pointed out in this section. It would be difficult to determine the direction you are heading without knowing whether or not you are succeeding in the first place. Project managers need to look at their product quality. Are they delivering the best quality product in the market? If yes, is this product getting to consumers at the right time? Beyond that, they should also look at customer satisfaction. Are customers satisfied with the product? Such metrics give project managers deeper insight into their performance levels. More importantly, they should seek to improve continuously as this is the best way to counter competition in the market.

Final Thoughts

Congratulations on getting to this section of the book. By now, you understand what agile project management is. Certainly, when managing projects, every manager yearns to make sure that their project succeeds. Unfortunately, most of them utilize a traditional approach to project management. This makes it difficult to deliver a product in the market which meets clients' needs. The agile method of project management is a new way of handling projects by promoting rapid change in the project development process. The agile method was introduced after software developers found it difficult to deliver their products in time when using the traditional approach. Using this technique, they delivered applications late, and sometimes, their projects were canceled. This happened because of the delays which affected the delivery of products in time.

Following the frustrations faced by software developers, they had to come up with a method which focused more on the product and not the process. They aimed to make sure that a product was in front of the consumers as quickly as possible. The fast delivery of software products was the only way that developers could understand what the customers wanted and make necessary changes. This is what led to Agile Project Management. Sure, the method was introduced to benefit software developers, but it can equally be utilized in any organization. The idea of managing projects occurs in every institution. Therefore, using the agile method can be an effective way to guarantee that a project succeeds.

Just as a reminder, the agile method has 12 principles which govern the way a project should be handled. The highest priority of an agile project is to meet customer requirements through rapid and continuous delivery. Also, the change should be acknowledged at all stages of the development process. The agile method also promotes the idea that the project is built around a group of motivated individuals. Therefore, no one needs to be pushed around to meet their daily targets.

When using the agile method, face-to-face interactions are regarded as the most effective form of communication. Technology has transformed how people communicate. There are social platforms that make it easy for people to interact regardless of their geographic location. Nonetheless, when using the agile method, face-to-face interactions are highly valued. This is the best way to get prompt feedback concerning the project's progress.

Additionally, an agile environment is all about simplicity. The project manager should work towards ensuring that any complexities in the development process are reduced. They should define every path in a way that makes it easy for the team to focus more on delivering a product that meets customer requirements. Don't forget; there are regular inspections at every stage of the product development process. This guarantees the effectiveness of a product in the eyes of a consumer.

But, it should be noted that the process of implementing the agile project management method is not as easy as it sounds. A project manager should be careful not to implement the method before understanding certain aspects of the organization, including their willingness to take risks, the agility levels of the team in place, and their risk-averseness. Knowing this sets the right platform to implement a method which will work with the organization. Without a doubt, it wouldn't be practical to use this strategy in an environment where the team is not agile. So, it is important to consider the aspects of the organization before taking any steps.

The implementation of the agile method not only requires the organization to create an agile environment but also to transform its mindset. You cannot have an agile environment when workers do not have an agile mindset. In this case, individuals in the organization should believe in the need for change. Equally, they should be flexible enough to adapt to fast changes. Transforming people's mindset also requires them to understand what the Agile Manifesto promotes. They should be well-informed about the four core values and the principles of the manifesto.

Equally, your organization needs an agile environment that supports an agile way of doing things. How can this be achieved? From the lessons learned, focus on people, the structure, and the process. Creating an agile environment begins by recruiting the right people to work on the project. The human resources department should understand that they should concentrate on the bigger picture when hiring people. Besides their skills, they should also consider their creativity and collaborativeness. Individuals should also be curious enough to try things out with other team members.

The structure of the organization must be carefully defined. The existing structure should not pose any complications in the process. For instance, the project manager should not find it difficult to make decisions without consulting with executives. The consultation process will drag down the business. A hierarchical structure might appear appealing, but in the real sense, it slows things down.

The agile project management process will not be complete without making use of agile tools. These are tools which have been designed to help you work efficiently. The significance of using these tools is that you get time to focus on what is more important in the development process. Remember, you need to work fast and adapt quickly to changes. This might not be possible if you go the manual way. Forget the idea of using paperwork to keep track of things. Numerous software products have been designed to automate the entire process. It is best that you know the right tool for you.

Popular agile tools which you might come across during your search include Clarizen, Trello, Jira, Taiga, and Pivotal Tracker. Before choosing a tool, always remember to go over its features. You could also test the product by using the trial period. Don't pay for a product which testing its functionality.

Yes, there are challenges that you will face while implementing the agile method. However, you should always focus on the bigger picture and reflect on the many benefits associated with it. The agile method of project management will always help you identify incorrect approaches with ease. Not to mention, the method promotes quick decision-making. This is possible through the collaborative environment in which your team works. Bear in mind that an agile environment also promotes a culture where change is embraced. Individuals get to understand that change is what makes the end product thrive in the market. Arguably, it is also through this change that people will be flexible to adjust quickly to the needs of the market.

Moreover, the project manager should not forget to measure how their agile systems are performing. This is the best way to improve continuously. Gauging their level of performance can be done by looking at the product quality. The end product they deliver to consumers should feature all the requirements expected. Besides delivering a high-quality product, timely delivery is imperative. Hence, their level of success can also be measured by considering whether or not they completed the product before the scheduled deadline. Other ways to measure success include looking at the product scope, project visibility, and the overall business value gained in using an agile system.

The agile project management method is quite compelling. There are many reasons to go the agile way. Forget about the conventional way of doing things. Today, consumers change their mind in a flip. Therefore, you need to be ready to adjust to such changes rapidly. Keep in mind that your ability to change will contribute a lot to the success of your product. It determines the type of product that you will release to the market. Of course, a product tailored to meet all the customer requirements will highly likely perform well, too. So, it makes a lot of sense to transform your way of managing projects. The agile method will lead your organization to succeed.

Good luck!